I0065542

How do I Become Rich

How Do I Become Rich? is a simple, step-by-step guide that reveals practical money habits anyone can use to build lasting wealth. Discover how to take control of your finances, grow your income, and finally achieve financial freedom.

Written by

ERIC LEBOUTHILLIER

AcraSolution | 2025 1st Edition
www.acrasolution.com

Preface

Who this book is for

- **Beginners** who want a clear starting point but feel overwhelmed by financial jargon.

- **Young adults** (college students, early professionals) who want to avoid debt traps and learn money skills early.

- **Everyday people** who live paycheck-to-paycheck and need simple, actionable steps to save and grow.

- Not for advanced investors or people already deep into complex finance strategies.

What to expect from this book

- **Foundations first:** Budgeting, saving, cutting unnecessary expenses.

- **Income growth basics:** Side hustles, skill-building, and realistic ways to boost earnings.

- **Wealth principles:** Why consistency, patience, and mindset matter more than "get rich quick."

- **Step-by-step guides:** Practical frameworks to apply immediately — not theory-heavy.

- **Realistic results:** Progress measured in **months and years**, not overnight.

LEGAL DISCLAIMER

This publication is intended solely for informational and educational purposes. It does not constitute legal, financial, medical, or professional advice. The content is not a substitute for consultation with qualified experts or licensed professionals in the relevant fields.

Portions of this work have been created or assisted by artificial intelligence (AI) tools. While every reasonable effort has been made to review, fact-check, and edit the content for clarity and accuracy, AI-generated information may occasionally contain errors, omissions, or generalized statements. The author and publisher do not guarantee the accuracy, completeness, or reliability of the information provided.

Readers are strongly encouraged to seek independent advice tailored to their personal circumstances from qualified legal, financial, healthcare, or compliance professionals before making decisions or taking action based on this content.

References to specific products, services, companies, websites, or technologies do not imply endorsement or affiliation unless explicitly stated. All trademarks and brand names mentioned remain the property of their respective owners.

The author and publisher disclaim any liability, loss, or risk incurred directly or indirectly from the use or misuse of this publication. This includes, but is not limited to, damages of any kind — including incidental, special, or consequential — arising out of the reliance on the material presented.

All references to laws, regulations, security standards, or industry guidelines are intended for general awareness only and may not reflect the most current legal developments. This publication is not intended to create, and receipt does not constitute, a client relationship with the author, publisher, or any affiliated entity.

By reading, accessing, or applying the content in this publication, you agree to do so at your own risk. If you do not accept these terms, you are advised to discontinue use of this material immediately.

Table of Contents

CHAPTER 1

Asking the Big Question: What Does "Rich" Really Mean?

The Difference Between Being Wealthy, Rich, and Financially Free

When most people say they want to be "rich," they often mean a mixture of things—having more money, living without financial stress, enjoying luxuries, or simply not having to worry about bills. But "rich" isn't the same as being wealthy, and neither guarantees financial freedom. Understanding the distinctions is critical, because without clarity, you might chase the wrong goal and end up dissatisfied—even if your bank account grows.

Being Rich: High Income, High Lifestyle

Being rich is often about **income and lifestyle**. A rich person earns a lot of money and spends a lot of money. They might live in a large home, drive luxury cars, and vacation in exotic places. But richness is fragile—it depends on the continuation of income. If the income stops, the lifestyle usually collapses.

Think of a highly paid surgeon earning $500,000 a year. They are undeniably rich. But if their expenses are $450,000 annually and their savings are minimal, they're one accident or career-ending injury away from financial trouble. The appearance of wealth doesn't equal security. Richness is more about **cash flow** than lasting stability.

This is why many celebrities who earn millions can still go bankrupt. They were rich, but not truly wealthy.

Being Wealthy: Assets and Time

Wealth, in contrast, is measured not just by money but by **time and ownership**. A wealthy person owns assets—businesses, investments, or properties—that generate income even when they are not actively working.

A helpful question to measure wealth is: *If you stopped working today, how long could you maintain your current lifestyle?* If the answer is months or years, you're building wealth. If the answer is days or weeks, you're only rich.

For example, imagine someone who owns several rental properties that generate $15,000 monthly in passive income. Even if they never worked again, those assets would continue to support their lifestyle. This is true wealth: the ability to sustain your life independent of active labor.

Wealth is not only about accumulation; it's about **sustainability**. It builds a foundation that allows freedom of choice, protection against economic shocks, and the possibility to pass something valuable to the next generation.

Financial Freedom: The Ultimate Goal

Financial freedom is a step beyond wealth. It is not just about having money, but about having **control**—the freedom to design your life without financial constraints dictating your choices.

Someone financially free may not own a yacht or a mansion, but they live on their terms. Their passive income exceeds their expenses, their debts are manageable or nonexistent, and they have peace of mind about money. They can choose to work because they want to, not because they have to.

For instance, a person who earns $60,000 annually from digital assets and lives on $40,000 a year is financially free, even if they don't fit the stereotypical image of "rich." Their life is flexible, their time is theirs, and their stress about money is minimal. That is true power.

Why the Distinction Matters

If you don't know the difference, you risk chasing an illusion. Many people chase "rich"—the cars, clothes, and expensive vacations—only to discover they feel trapped. They earn more, but they spend more. They upgrade their lifestyle but not their freedom.

Others focus on wealth-building but never align it with the life they want. They accumulate assets but continue living in scarcity, never granting themselves permission to enjoy what they've built.

Financial freedom ties both together. It balances income, assets, and personal values into a system where money becomes a tool, not a trap.

The Takeaway

Being rich is about income. Being wealthy is about assets and sustainability. Financial freedom is about control and choice. The sooner you clarify which of these you're truly aiming for, the sooner you can align your actions with that vision.

Growth begins not by chasing more, but by defining what "enough" means to you. Once you stop confusing wealth with richness, you can start building a life where money serves you—not the other way around.

Common Myths That Keep People Poor

Money is not just numbers on a spreadsheet—it's a belief system. The way you think about money shapes the way you earn, save, and invest it. Unfortunately, many people grow up surrounded by myths about money that feel true but silently sabotage their financial future. If you don't unlearn these myths, you'll carry them like invisible chains, even when opportunities to grow are right in front of you.

Myth 1: "Making More Money Will Solve My Problems"

It's tempting to believe that higher income is the cure for financial stress. But countless stories prove otherwise. Many people double or triple their income and remain stuck in debt because their **spending grows faster than their earnings**. This is called **lifestyle inflation**—the more you make, the more you feel entitled to spend.

Consider lottery winners. Statistics show that nearly 70% of them lose all their winnings within a few years. Their income skyrocketed, but their habits stayed the same—or got worse. Without financial discipline, no amount of money is enough.

The truth: money magnifies your habits. If you manage $1,000 poorly, you'll likely manage $100,000 the same way.

Myth 2: "Debt Is Always Bad"

Many people avoid debt at all costs, believing it's inherently negative. While **bad debt**—like high-interest credit cards—can trap you, **good debt**—like a loan for an appreciating asset or business investment—can accelerate growth.

A person who avoids all debt might miss opportunities, such as buying property that generates passive income. The key is not to fear debt, but to learn how to **use it strategically**. Wealthy people don't avoid debt; they master it.

Myth 3: "I'll Start Saving When I Make More"

This myth keeps people locked in a cycle of waiting. If you can't save when you earn $2,000 a month, you won't magically save when you earn $10,000. Saving is not about the amount—it's about the discipline of **paying yourself first**, no matter how small the amount.

For example, setting aside just $50 monthly at age 20 and investing it can grow into six figures by retirement, thanks to compounding. Waiting until you "make enough" is just procrastination in disguise.

Myth 4: "Rich People Got Lucky"

This belief comforts those who feel stuck, but it removes personal responsibility. While luck and privilege can play roles, most wealth is built through **knowledge, persistence, and calculated risk-taking**.

Think of entrepreneurs who failed multiple times before succeeding. Or immigrants who arrive with little but build businesses through consistent effort. By dismissing wealth as luck, you unconsciously excuse yourself from learning the skills and strategies that could change your financial life.

Myth 5: "Money Is the Root of All Evil"

This mindset creates guilt around financial success. In reality, money is neutral—it simply amplifies the values of the person who holds it. A generous person with money can fund schools, medical care, or clean water projects. A selfish person with money might misuse it. The difference is not the money—it's the mindset.

If you believe money is evil, you'll unconsciously repel it. If you see money as a tool, you'll attract and use it with purpose.

The Takeaway

Poverty isn't just about a lack of money—it's about a lack of accurate financial beliefs. Myths are comfortable, but they cost you growth. To move toward financial freedom, you must unlearn these inherited limitations and replace them with truths: more income doesn't guarantee security, good debt can create opportunities, saving is a discipline, wealth is built—not just luck—and money is a tool, not a villain.

Growth starts when you stop treating money like a mystery and start treating it like a skill you can learn.

How Mindset Shapes Your Financial Reality

Money doesn't just live in your wallet or bank account—it lives in your head first. Your beliefs, emotions, and habits around money create the invisible script that dictates your financial outcomes. Some people call it a "money mindset." Whether you realize it or not, this mindset determines whether you move toward financial freedom or stay stuck in cycles of stress and scarcity.

The Psychology of Money Scripts

From childhood, you absorb financial beliefs from family, culture, and society. If you grew up hearing "money doesn't grow on trees," you might see money as scarce and difficult to earn. If your parents argued about bills, you may associate money with conflict. Psychologists call these **money scripts**—unconscious beliefs that drive financial behaviors.

For instance, one person might overspend to "treat themselves" because they associate money with pleasure and self-worth. Another may hoard money excessively out of fear, never enjoying what they've earned. Both extremes are shaped by mindset, not reality.

Scarcity vs. Abundance Thinking

Two primary mindsets dominate financial behavior: **scarcity** and **abundance**.

- **Scarcity mindset** sees money as limited. People with this mindset think, "If they have more, I'll have less." This thinking often leads to fear-based decisions: hoarding, avoiding risks, or underinvesting in opportunities.

- **Abundance mindset** sees money as renewable. People with this mindset believe, "Opportunities are everywhere, and I can create more." This fosters creativity, generosity, and long-term wealth-building.

Consider two entrepreneurs with the same $5,000. The scarcity thinker clings to it, afraid to lose. The abundance thinker invests it in learning, marketing, or a scalable project. Over time, the latter multiplies their money, while the former watches inflation erode theirs.

The Role of Self-Worth

Your financial ceiling often mirrors your self-worth. If deep down you don't believe you deserve wealth, you'll unconsciously sabotage yourself. This could look like undercharging for your work, avoiding promotions, or hesitating to invest.

Take freelancers, for example. Many underprice their services not because their skills are weak, but because they fear rejection. The result? They work harder for less, reinforcing the belief that money is scarce. Shifting their mindset to "I provide value worth paying for" often changes their income dramatically without changing their skill set.

Reframing Failure and Risk

Wealthy people don't see failure as final; they see it as feedback. A scarcity mindset avoids risks, fearing loss. An abundance mindset embraces calculated risks, knowing failure teaches lessons that often lead to bigger wins.

Thomas Edison famously said he didn't fail a thousand times when inventing the lightbulb—he discovered a thousand ways that didn't work. Apply this mindset to money: every failed side hustle, rejected job application, or poor investment can become data that sharpens your strategy.

Training Your Money Mindset

The good news: mindset is not fixed. You can rewire it. Practical steps include:

1. **Awareness** – Write down your inherited money beliefs. Which serve you, and which limit you?
2. **Reframe** – Replace negative scripts with empowering truths. Change "I'll never get ahead" to "I can learn the skills to build wealth."
3. **Exposure** – Surround yourself with examples of financial success. Books, mentors, and communities normalize abundance thinking.
4. **Practice** – Small daily actions, like saving $10 or investing modestly, reinforce a new identity: someone who grows wealth.

The Takeaway

Your financial reality is not just shaped by your paycheck—it's shaped by your perspective. Scarcity keeps you fearful and stagnant. Abundance keeps you creative and resilient. When you change your beliefs, you change your behavior. And when you change your behavior, your bank account eventually follows.

Growth begins in the mind. Master your money mindset, and you'll unlock doors that strategies alone can't open.

Defining Your Version of "Rich" Before Chasing It

Many people sprint toward the idea of being "rich" without ever stopping to ask: *What does rich actually mean to me?* They adopt someone else's dream—a luxury car, a big house, a certain number in the bank—without questioning whether those goals align with their values. The danger is clear: if you chase someone else's definition of success, you can reach the finish line and still feel empty.

Clarity is power. Until you define your version of "rich," you risk wasting years climbing a ladder that's leaning against the wrong wall.

The Trap of Comparison

Social media intensifies the confusion. One scroll shows a twenty-year-old influencer traveling the world, another shows a tech founder celebrating a million-dollar exit. The subconscious message is: *This is what rich looks like.*

But comparison creates financial anxiety. A teacher earning $60,000 might feel "poor" when compared to a celebrity, but "rich" compared to global averages. Richness, then, is not an absolute—it's relative. Unless you anchor it to your own values, you'll always feel behind.

Redefining Rich in Terms of Freedom

For some, rich means a seven-figure bank account. For others, it means working four hours a day and spending the rest of the time with family. The **common denominator** is freedom—the ability to design life on your terms.

Imagine two people:

- Person A earns $500,000 a year but works 80-hour weeks in a job they dislike.
- Person B earns $80,000 a year remotely, with flexible hours and enough savings to travel regularly.

Who is richer? By society's default definition, Person A. But by the measure of freedom and fulfillment, Person B may be far wealthier.

Aligning Rich With Your Values

Money itself doesn't create happiness—alignment does. If your version of rich means traveling, then investing in experiences may bring more fulfillment than buying a mansion. If your version of rich means security, then building a solid investment portfolio may feel better than owning flashy cars.

Practical exercise: Write down your **Top 5 values** (e.g., family, creativity, adventure, health, contribution). Then, describe what a "rich life" would look like if each of those values were fully expressed. This reframes richness from a vague goal into a specific vision that guides your financial choices.

Setting a Number, But Not the Wrong One

It's useful to define a target number—whether that's $100,000 in savings, $1M net worth, or $5,000 monthly passive income. But the number should serve your life vision, not the other way around. Too many people chase higher numbers endlessly, thinking the next milestone will finally bring peace.

Research in behavioral economics shows that happiness rises with income only up to a point—enough to meet needs and reduce stress. Beyond that, fulfillment depends less on money and more on purpose, relationships, and freedom of choice.

The Takeaway

Defining your version of rich is not about rejecting wealth—it's about directing it. When you tie your financial goals to your values, you gain clarity. You stop chasing status symbols and start building a life that feels rich on your terms.

Growth is not about copying someone else's dream. It's about creating your own definition of "rich," then using money as a tool to make it real.

CHAPTER 2

The Foundations of Wealth

The Money Equation: Earn More, Spend Less, Invest the Rest

Every financial system, no matter how complex it looks, boils down to a simple equation:

Income – Expenses = What You Keep → Invested = Wealth

This formula is deceptively simple. Yet most people ignore it, chasing hacks, trends, or luck. The truth is, unless you master this equation, no investment strategy or side hustle will rescue you. Building wealth starts with discipline in this basic flow: earn more, spend less, and invest the rest.

Step 1: Earn More

There is a ceiling to how much you can cut expenses, but there is no ceiling to how much you can earn. That's why wealth creation often begins with finding ways to expand income.

Consider two friends: Alex saves 20% of a $40,000 salary, while Jordan saves 20% of a $100,000 salary. Even with the same discipline, Jordan builds wealth more than twice as fast.

Earning more can mean negotiating raises, developing new skills, starting a side hustle, or building passive income streams. It requires initiative and often discomfort—stepping out of routine, learning new things, or taking risks. But income growth is the fuel that accelerates the wealth equation.

Step 2: Spend Less

Here's where many stumble. High income doesn't guarantee wealth if expenses grow just as fast. The difference between someone who becomes wealthy and someone who stays broke often lies in one word: **discipline.**

Spending less doesn't mean living joylessly. It means living consciously. Every dollar you spend should be aligned with your values and your version of "rich." That $200 designer shirt might feel good in the moment, but if your long-term goal is travel freedom, that same $200 invested could pay for future experiences.

Small leaks sink big ships. Even trimming daily habits—like replacing a $7 coffee habit with a $2 homemade version—can free thousands annually to invest.

Step 3: Invest the Rest

Saving alone is not enough. Inflation silently erodes cash, turning today's $100 into tomorrow's $80 in value. To grow wealth, you must **invest what you keep**.

Investing transforms money into an employee that works 24/7, even while you sleep. Whether it's stocks, real estate, or businesses, the principle is the same: assets generate more income, which compounds over time.

The earlier you invest, the more time compounding has to work in your favor. A 25-year-old investing $500 a month at a modest return can retire a millionaire. A 45-year-old starting with the same strategy will struggle to catch up. Time is the invisible multiplier.

The Balance Between the Three

Focusing only on one step creates imbalance:

- **Only earning more** can lead to lifestyle inflation.
- **Only cutting expenses** can trap you in a scarcity mindset.
- **Only investing without income growth** may limit your potential.

The power comes from applying all three together. Earn more to expand your possibilities, spend less to protect your margin, and invest the rest to build lasting wealth.

A Real-World Illustration

Imagine Sarah earns $60,000 a year. She reduces expenses to live on $40,000, freeing $20,000 to invest annually. If she invests wisely at an average 7% return, she'll have over $1 million in about 25 years.

Now imagine David, who earns $100,000 but spends $98,000. Despite his higher income, he only saves $2,000 annually. In 25 years, he has less than $150,000. Sarah, with less income, wins because she applied the money equation with discipline.

The Takeaway

Wealth is not an accident—it's math applied consistently. Earn more, spend less, and invest the rest. This simple equation, executed over years, turns ordinary people into millionaires while those chasing shortcuts stay broke.

Growth doesn't come from complexity. It comes from applying timeless principles relentlessly.

Understanding Assets vs. Liabilities (Rich Dad 101 Made Practical)

One of the simplest yet most powerful financial lessons comes from Robert Kiyosaki's *Rich Dad Poor Dad*: the difference between an **asset** and a **liability.** At first glance, it sounds obvious—assets are "good," liabilities are "bad." But most people misclassify them, and that misunderstanding is what keeps them stuck.

Wealthy people focus on buying and building assets. The middle class and poor often pile up liabilities disguised as "investments." Let's strip away the confusion and make this distinction practical.

Assets: What Puts Money in Your Pocket

An **asset** is anything that generates income or increases in value over time. Assets work for you instead of against you. They either:

1. Provide **cash flow** (rental income, dividends, royalties), or
2. Appreciate in **value** (stocks, real estate, businesses).

Examples:

- A rental property that pays you monthly.
- A portfolio of index funds that grows and pays dividends.
- A side business that produces profits.
- Intellectual property—like a book or app—that earns royalties.

Assets don't just look valuable on paper; they actively contribute to your wealth.

Liabilities: What Takes Money Out of Your Pocket

A **liability** is anything that costs you money to maintain, even if it looks like an asset. Many people confuse "ownership" with "investment." Just because you own something doesn't make it an asset.

Examples:

- A car with monthly payments, insurance, and maintenance costs.
- A large house with high mortgage, taxes, and upkeep (unless it produces rental income).
- Credit card debt that grows with interest.

- Consumer gadgets bought on loans.

These items may bring comfort or status, but financially, they drain cash flow.

The Big Misconception: "My House Is an Asset"

This is one of the most common mistakes. People call their personal home an asset, but in financial terms, it's often a liability. Why? Because it costs money every month—mortgage, repairs, taxes—and doesn't generate income.

Now, a property can be both. If you rent out part of your home (like Airbnb) and it generates income greater than its expenses, that portion is an asset. Otherwise, it's a liability you happen to live in.

How Wealthy People Think Differently

The wealthy ask a simple question before buying: *Will this put money in my pocket or take it out?*

- When they buy cars, they look for ways to offset costs (leasing for business deductions, or renting them out occasionally).
- When they buy properties, they focus on rental yield, not curb appeal.
- When they spend, they often tie it back to income generation.

This doesn't mean you should never buy liabilities. Comfort and enjoyment have value. The point is awareness: know the difference, and prioritize assets first.

Shifting Your Buying Decisions

Practical application: Next time you're about to make a big purchase, pause and classify it—asset or liability? If it's a liability, ask: *Am I willing to sacrifice future wealth for this today?*

Sometimes the answer is yes, but often, this pause alone changes behavior.

Instead of financing a luxury car, maybe you invest in dividend-paying stocks that cover the cost of a modest car. Over time, the asset grows, and later you can afford the luxury without sabotaging your future.

The Takeaway

The rich grow wealth by multiplying assets. The poor and middle class stay stuck by multiplying liabilities while convincing themselves they're building wealth.

Growth begins when you see money for what it does, not just what it buys. Assets feed your future. Liabilities starve it. Choose accordingly.

Building Your First Emergency Fund

Before you invest in stocks, real estate, or any wealth-building strategy, you need a safety net. That safety net is your **emergency fund**—a cash reserve set aside for life's unexpected events.

Without it, even small crises can derail your finances. A car repair, medical bill, or job loss can force you into debt, undoing months or years of progress. With it, you gain stability, confidence, and the freedom to make smarter financial moves without constant fear of "what if?"

Why an Emergency Fund Comes First

Many people rush into investing before saving an emergency cushion. The problem? If life throws a surprise expense, they're forced to pull money out of investments at the worst time, often at a loss.

For example: Imagine you invest $5,000 in the stock market but have no savings. If your car breaks down, you might need that $5,000 immediately. If the market is down, you sell at a loss. An emergency fund prevents this by covering short-term needs so your long-term investments remain untouched.

How Much Do You Need?

Financial planners often recommend **3–6 months of essential expenses**. For someone spending $2,000 a month, that's $6,000–$12,000 saved. If your job is unstable, you might aim for more. If you have multiple income streams or strong job security, 3 months may be enough.

The key word is *essential*. Don't calculate based on luxury spending. Focus on rent, food, utilities, transportation, insurance, and medical costs—the basics that keep life running.

Where to Keep It

Your emergency fund should be:

- **Safe** – not exposed to market risk.
- **Accessible** – easy to withdraw quickly when needed.
- **Separate** – not mixed with spending accounts, so you're not tempted to dip into it.

The best places:

- High-yield savings accounts.
- Money market accounts.
- Short-term certificates of deposit (if you can lock in without penalties).

Avoid risky investments or tying the money up in assets you can't access quickly, like real estate. Remember, this fund isn't meant to grow wealth; it's meant to **protect** it.

Starting Small, Building Consistently

For many, saving 3–6 months of expenses feels overwhelming. Start smaller. Aim for $500 first—enough to cover most unexpected bills. Then grow to $1,000, then one month, then three. Breaking it down makes the goal achievable.

One strategy: automate the process. Set up a recurring transfer of even $50–$100 a week into a separate savings account. Over time, it builds faster than you expect, and you don't feel the daily burden of saving large chunks.

The Emotional Side of an Emergency Fund

The benefits are not just financial—they're psychological. Knowing you have a buffer reduces stress, increases confidence, and helps you make rational financial decisions instead of panic-driven ones. People with emergency funds report greater financial well-being, even if their incomes are modest.

Think of it as buying peace of mind. That security allows you to take calculated risks in your career, business, or investments without constant anxiety.

The Takeaway

Your emergency fund is your foundation. It won't make you rich, but it will keep you from becoming poor when life happens. Build it before you invest aggressively, and you'll give yourself both protection and freedom.

Growth isn't only about chasing opportunity—it's also about shielding yourself from setbacks. An emergency fund does exactly that.

Why Financial Literacy Is the True Starting Point

Earning money is important. Saving money is important. But without understanding how money actually works, you will always be at risk of losing it. That's why financial literacy—the ability to understand and apply financial knowledge—is the true starting point of wealth.

Think of money like a language. If you don't speak it, you'll always depend on translators—bankers, advisors, friends, or worse, salespeople who don't have your best interests at heart. But once you become fluent, you gain independence. You stop guessing and start making informed decisions.

What Financial Literacy Really Means

Financial literacy isn't about becoming an accountant or stock market expert. It's about grasping the **core principles** that guide smart money decisions:

- **Budgeting** – knowing where your money goes.
- **Debt management** – understanding interest and avoiding traps.
- **Investing basics** – compounding, risk, diversification.
- **Taxes** – how they impact your income and investments.
- **Insurance** – protecting against life's biggest risks.

These fundamentals might seem boring compared to flashy "get rich quick" ideas, but they're what separate financial stability from financial chaos.

Why Lack of Literacy Keeps People Stuck

Most schools don't teach personal finance. As a result, people learn about money through trial and error—or from family and friends who may not be financially literate themselves. This creates cycles of poor money habits passed down like heirlooms.

Take credit cards. Many people don't realize that carrying a balance means paying **20% interest or more**—essentially giving banks free profits while staying stuck in debt. Or consider taxes: without basic tax knowledge, people miss legal deductions that could save them thousands annually.

Ignorance is expensive.

Knowledge Turns Into Confidence

The biggest advantage of financial literacy is not just making better choices—it's the confidence it creates. When you know how money works, you stop fearing it. You can evaluate opportunities, negotiate better, and resist scams.

Imagine two people offered the same investment. One has no literacy and feels overwhelmed, so they either avoid it entirely (missing out) or jump in blindly (risking loss). The other understands risk, diversification, and returns, so they can analyze and decide wisely. Same opportunity—different outcome.

How to Start Building Literacy

You don't need an MBA. You need consistent learning in small doses. Practical steps include:

1. **Books** – classics like *Rich Dad Poor Dad* or *The Millionaire Next Door* for mindset, and more technical guides like *The Intelligent Investor* for investing.

2. **Podcasts and courses** – free or affordable resources that simplify money topics.
3. **Practice** – the best teacher. Start a budget, track expenses, open a small investment account. Experience reinforces knowledge.
4. **Mentors and communities** – surround yourself with financially aware people; their habits will rub off.

The Takeaway

Financial literacy is the foundation that supports every other step toward wealth. Without it, high income can vanish, assets can be mismanaged, and investments can backfire. With it, even modest income can grow steadily into financial freedom.

Growth begins with understanding. When you master the basics of money, you're no longer playing blind—you're playing to win.

CHAPTER 3

Earning More: The Modern Income Playbook

Active Income: Jobs, Side Hustles, Freelancing

The first and most familiar form of income is **active income**—money you earn by trading your time and skills for payment. It's the paycheck from your job, the fee from a freelance gig, or the profit from a side hustle. For most people, this is the starting point of wealth creation.

Active income is powerful because it's immediate. You put in effort, and you get money in return. But it's also limited because it depends on your time and energy. The key is learning how to maximize active income and then using it as a springboard toward more sustainable wealth.

The Role of a Job

A job is often seen as a trap, but it doesn't have to be. It can be a tool. For beginners, a steady paycheck provides security, structure, and a platform for skill development. Many successful entrepreneurs and investors started by leveraging their jobs to gain experience, build savings, and create networks.

However, relying solely on a job can be risky. Layoffs, corporate restructuring, or health issues can wipe out your income overnight. This is why it's important to supplement a job with other forms of active income.

The Power of Side Hustles

A side hustle is a way to earn beyond your main job. It could be anything from driving for a ride-share company to tutoring, selling products online, or running a weekend service business.

The beauty of side hustles is flexibility. They allow you to experiment with entrepreneurship on a small scale, test markets, and develop new skills without the risk of quitting your job.

Real-world example: John, a software engineer, starts building websites for small businesses on weekends. Within two years, his side hustle grows enough to match his salary, giving him the option to leave his job—or simply enjoy double income.

Freelancing: Owning Your Skills

Freelancing sits between traditional employment and entrepreneurship. Instead of working for one employer, you sell your skills directly to clients. This can mean writing, design, programming, consulting, or dozens of other services.

The advantage of freelancing is control—you set your rates, choose your projects, and expand your client base. The challenge is inconsistency. Some months may bring high earnings, while others may feel dry. That's why successful freelancers treat it like a business: marketing themselves, diversifying clients, and managing cash flow carefully.

Multiplying Your Active Income

Here's where strategy comes in:

1. **Skill stacking** – Combine multiple skills to charge more. For example, a graphic designer who also knows copywriting can offer a more valuable package than either skill alone.
2. **Negotiation** – Many employees never ask for raises. Research shows those who negotiate salaries consistently earn significantly more over their careers.
3. **Time leverage** – Use tools and systems to reduce hours while maintaining income. Automating parts of your side hustle (like using templates, outsourcing tasks, or digital tools) increases efficiency.

Turning Active Income Into Wealth

The danger of active income is mistaking it for wealth. Remember: as soon as you stop working, active income stops. That's why it must be seen as **fuel**—the money you earn actively should be funneled into building assets and passive income streams.

A side hustle that pays $1,000 a month is valuable. But if you invest that $1,000 consistently into compounding assets, in a decade it could grow into six figures—something no one-time hustle can match.

The Takeaway

Active income is the first step, not the final destination. Jobs, side hustles, and freelancing can fund your lifestyle, accelerate debt repayment, and build the capital to invest. But they should be seen as tools, not traps.

Growth comes when you stop asking, *How much can I earn today?* and start asking, *How can I use today's earnings to buy tomorrow's freedom?*

Passive Income: Royalties, Online Content, Rental, Dividends

If active income is trading time for money, **passive income** is the opposite: setting up systems, assets, or intellectual property that continue to generate money with little to no daily effort. It's the holy grail of wealth creation because it buys you the most valuable resource—**time**.

Passive income is not magic. It often requires upfront effort, investment, or creativity. But once established, it frees you from the constant cycle of "work more to earn more."

Royalties: Getting Paid for Ideas

Royalties are payments you earn when others use something you created. This could be a book, a song, a patent, or even software.

For example, an author writes a book once but earns royalties for years every time it sells. A musician records an album and collects income every time it streams. An inventor patents a product and gets paid whenever companies use the design.

Royalties reward creativity and intellectual property. They take effort to establish, but they can turn knowledge or talent into long-term financial streams.

Online Content: Digital Assets That Scale

The digital world has exploded with opportunities for passive income. YouTube channels, podcasts, online courses, and blogs can all generate revenue through ads, subscriptions, or product sales.

Unlike traditional businesses, digital assets scale globally with low cost. A single online course filmed once can be sold to thousands of students. A YouTube video posted today can keep earning ad revenue years later.

Consider Ali Abdaal, a doctor who started a YouTube channel to share productivity tips. Over time, his content generated millions in ad revenue, course sales, and sponsorships—proving that consistent content creation can evolve into a passive income empire.

Rental Income: Property That Pays You

Real estate is one of the oldest forms of passive income. A rental property generates monthly cash flow while typically appreciating in value over time.

For example, buying a small apartment, covering the mortgage through rent, and pocketing the difference creates consistent income. Over decades, rising property values add another layer of wealth.

Of course, rentals require capital and management. But tools like property managers and platforms such as Airbnb make it increasingly accessible—even for beginners.

Dividends: Owning Pieces of Companies

When you own stocks of dividend-paying companies, you earn a share of their profits. Unlike active income, you don't have to show up at the office to get paid. The company does the work; you collect the reward.

Dividend investing is particularly powerful because you can reinvest dividends to buy more shares, compounding your income year after year. It's slow at first, but over time, the snowball effect can be life-changing.

For instance, someone who invests $500 a month in dividend stocks for 20 years could build a portfolio generating thousands in yearly passive income—without lifting a finger beyond the initial investments.

The Myth of "Truly Passive"

It's important to be realistic: very few income streams are completely effortless. Writing a book requires months of work. A rental property requires occasional maintenance. A YouTube channel requires ongoing creativity.

The difference is **leverage**. Instead of working every hour to earn every dollar, you put in effort once and keep reaping returns long after. Passive income is not about zero work—it's about **asymmetry**: small input, ongoing output.

The Takeaway

Active income builds your foundation. Passive income builds your freedom. Whether through royalties, online content, rentals, or dividends, passive streams turn money and effort into systems that keep working when you don't.

Growth comes when you stop asking, *How do I work harder?* and start asking, *How can I build something that keeps working without me?*

The Rise of Digital Wealth: AI, Automation, Online Businesses

Wealth used to be built slowly through traditional paths: decades in a career, saving diligently, and investing cautiously. Today, technology has rewritten the rules. For the first time in history, individuals can create wealth at scale without massive capital, connections, or gatekeepers. The digital economy—powered by AI, automation, and online platforms—has lowered the barriers to entry and opened doors to anyone willing to learn and adapt.

From Factories to Laptops

A century ago, wealth came from factories, land, or industrial empires—things that required enormous capital. Today, many businesses run from a laptop. A teenager with Wi-Fi can sell products globally, build a personal brand, or leverage AI to automate tasks that once required teams of employees.

Consider Shopify stores, YouTube channels, or digital product businesses. These models don't require physical storefronts or inventory. Instead, they scale digitally, reaching millions without traditional overhead.

AI as the New Leverage

Artificial Intelligence is the most powerful tool of leverage today. Tasks that once took hours—copywriting, graphic design, video editing, coding—can now be accelerated or partially automated with AI tools.

For entrepreneurs, this means higher efficiency, lower costs, and faster experimentation. A solo creator can now achieve what once required a small company. For employees, AI literacy can dramatically increase value, opening doors to higher-paying roles.

Example: A marketer who uses AI to automate ad campaigns, analyze customer data, and generate creative ideas can outperform entire traditional marketing teams. That advantage often translates directly into higher income.

Online Businesses That Scale

Three categories of online businesses dominate the modern wealth landscape:

1. **E-commerce** – Selling physical or digital products globally with platforms like Amazon, Etsy, or Shopify.
2. **Content-driven businesses** – Monetizing attention through YouTube, podcasts, blogs, and social media.
3. **Knowledge-based businesses** – Turning expertise into courses, coaching, or subscription communities.

Each model allows you to build assets that compound—audiences, customer bases, and intellectual property. Unlike freelancing or jobs, these businesses are scalable. You put in effort once, and technology enables you to serve thousands or millions simultaneously.

Automation: The Silent Partner

Automation tools—email marketing systems, customer service bots, scheduling software—are silent partners that reduce the need for constant human input. For small business owners, this means freedom. Instead of spending hours on repetitive tasks, they can focus on growth, creativity, or simply reclaiming time.

For example, an online course creator can set up automated sales funnels. Once built, the system sells, delivers, and even follows up with customers 24/7—without the creator's daily involvement.

The Opportunity and the Challenge

The digital economy has democratized wealth creation, but it has also increased competition. While opportunities are abundant, so is noise. Success requires differentiation—clear branding, authentic voice, or unique value.

It also requires resilience. Online businesses often grow slowly at first, with little visible reward. The compounding effect shows up later, rewarding persistence.

The Takeaway

The rise of digital wealth is not a passing trend—it's the new foundation of opportunity. AI, automation, and online platforms give ordinary people extraordinary leverage. But the tools alone don't make you rich. Your mindset, creativity, and persistence do.

Growth today doesn't require permission—it requires participation. The digital economy is here. The only question is whether you'll consume it passively or create within it actively.

Scaling Income Streams Instead of Relying on One

Most people are taught to depend on a single source of income: their job. This works fine—until it doesn't. Layoffs, health issues, or industry changes can wipe out a paycheck overnight. True financial security doesn't come from one stream of income, no matter how large. It comes from **multiple streams that protect and reinforce each other.**

Wealthy people don't ask, *How do I make more money from one source?* They ask, *How do I create systems that multiply income without multiplying effort?*

The Fragility of One Stream

Imagine a stool with one leg. It can stand if perfectly balanced, but it's unstable and easy to topple. Now imagine a stool with three or four legs. Even if one leg weakens, the stool holds steady. That's the difference between one income stream and several.

In 2008, when the financial crisis hit, millions of employees who relied solely on salaries were devastated. In contrast, those with multiple streams—dividends, rental income, side businesses—often survived or even thrived.

What Scaling Really Means

Scaling isn't about working more hours—it's about designing income that grows beyond your personal time.

- **Active scaling** – Raising rates, improving skills, or adding clients in freelancing or business.
- **Semi-passive scaling** – Creating systems or hiring people to handle parts of your business, freeing you to expand.

- **Passive scaling** – Building assets like online courses, royalties, investments, or real estate that grow without additional effort.

The goal is to shift gradually from income tied directly to your time toward income that compounds and multiplies independently.

Layering Streams Strategically

Not all income streams are equal. Some require upfront capital (real estate), some require time (freelancing), and others require creativity (online content). The smartest approach is layering: start with one reliable base, then add complementary streams.

Example:

- Base income: a stable job or freelance work.
- Secondary stream: a side hustle like consulting or digital products.
- Long-term stream: investments in stocks, index funds, or rentals.

Over time, these layers create resilience. If one stream slows, others keep flowing.

From Survival to Freedom

Multiple income streams aren't just about protection—they're about acceleration. Imagine you earn $60,000 from a job, $10,000 from freelancing, $5,000 from dividends, and $12,000 from an online business annually. That's $87,000 total—without being tied to one employer or market.

At that point, you don't just survive—you gain freedom. You can leave toxic jobs, take sabbaticals, or reinvest aggressively. Money stops being a leash and starts becoming a launchpad.

The Takeaway

Depending on one paycheck is financial fragility. Scaling income streams builds resilience, flexibility, and speed on the path to wealth. Each new stream adds a layer of security and opportunity.

Growth is not about working harder on one track. It's about building several tracks so your money journey continues even if one roadblocks.

CHAPTER 4

Mastering Money Habits

Budgeting Made Simple: 50/30/20 and Beyond

Budgeting has a reputation for being restrictive, like a financial diet. But at its core, budgeting isn't about deprivation—it's about direction. It's a plan that ensures your money serves your goals instead of slipping away unnoticed.

The challenge is that most people overcomplicate budgeting or avoid it entirely. The truth? A simple framework can provide clarity, flexibility, and control without drowning you in spreadsheets.

The 50/30/20 Rule

One of the most effective and beginner-friendly methods is the **50/30/20 rule**:

- **50%** of income for essentials: housing, food, transportation, bills.
- **30%** for wants: dining out, entertainment, travel, hobbies.
- **20%** for savings and debt repayment.

This model works because it balances responsibility with enjoyment. It prevents the all-or-nothing trap where people either overspend recklessly or live so frugally they burn out.

Example: If you earn $3,000 monthly after taxes, $1,500 covers essentials, $900 goes to wants, and $600 builds savings or reduces debt. Simple, clear, and sustainable.

Why Simplicity Wins

Budgeting fails when it feels like punishment. People set unrealistic limits, track every penny, and eventually give up. The 50/30/20 rule simplifies decisions, creates boundaries, and still leaves room for enjoyment.

Think of it like lanes on a highway. You don't need to measure every inch—you just need guardrails to stay on course.

Going Beyond 50/30/20

As your financial situation evolves, you can adjust the ratios. Some examples:

- **Aggressive savings phase** – 40/20/40 (living lean to save or invest heavily).
- **High-debt phase** – 50/20/30 (prioritizing debt repayment over wants).
- **Financial freedom phase** – 30/20/50 (once assets cover essentials, most income is reinvested).

The point is flexibility. Your budget should adapt to your goals, not trap you in a one-size-fits-all formula.

Tools That Make It Easy

Technology has eliminated most excuses for not budgeting. Apps like Mint, YNAB (You Need a Budget), or even simple bank alerts categorize spending automatically. You don't need to log every transaction manually. You just need visibility.

Another approach is the **envelope method**—digitally or physically. Divide money into "buckets" for each category. Once a bucket is empty, you stop spending in that area. This prevents overspending without constant micromanagement.

The Psychology of Budgeting

Budgeting isn't just math—it's mindset. It forces you to confront trade-offs. If you choose to spend $500 on dining out, you're also choosing not to invest that $500. Awareness creates accountability.

Over time, budgeting rewires habits. You begin to see spending not as random events, but as conscious choices aligned with your definition of "rich."

The Takeaway

Budgeting isn't about restriction—it's about control. Frameworks like 50/30/20 simplify the process, while adjustments and tools make it adaptable. With a clear budget, every dollar has a purpose, and every choice moves you closer to freedom.

Growth doesn't come from earning more alone—it comes from mastering how you direct what you already have.

Eliminating Debt Traps: Credit Cards, Bad Loans

Debt itself isn't evil—it's a tool. But like any tool, when misused, it can cause damage. Unfortunately, most people fall into **debt traps** that drain their income, erode their freedom, and keep them from building wealth.

These traps are designed. Credit card companies, payday lenders, and predatory loan services profit when you stay stuck in cycles of repayment. To escape, you must understand how these traps work and how to break free.

The Psychology Behind Debt Traps

Debt is tempting because it offers instant gratification. You want something now, and credit lets you have it without waiting. But the hidden cost is future income. Every time you swipe without the ability to pay in full, you're borrowing from tomorrow to fund today.

Companies know this. That's why credit cards offer rewards, points, and flashy perks—disguising high-interest rates that quietly eat away at your future.

Credit Cards: Convenience or Chains?

Used responsibly, credit cards can be tools—building credit history, offering fraud protection, and even providing rewards. But carried balances turn them into chains.

Most credit cards charge **15–25% interest annually**. That means a $1,000 balance can balloon into $2,000 in just three years if unpaid. Compare that to average investment returns (6–8%), and it's clear: credit card debt destroys wealth far faster than investing builds it.

The rule: If you can't pay the balance in full each month, the card is a liability, not a tool.

Bad Loans: When Borrowing Becomes a Trap

Not all loans are bad. Mortgages, student loans (used wisely), and business loans can be investments in assets or future income. **Bad loans**, however, are those that finance depreciating items or come with predatory terms.

Examples:

- Payday loans with outrageous fees.
- Car loans on vehicles that lose value the second you drive them off the lot.
- Personal loans for consumption, not investment.

These loans often come with interest so high that repayment feels endless, keeping you financially paralyzed.

Breaking Free: Debt Repayment Strategies

Escaping debt traps requires both mindset and method. Two proven strategies are:

1. **Debt Snowball** – Pay off the smallest debts first to build momentum and confidence, while making minimum payments on larger ones. Once one debt is gone, roll that payment into the next.
2. **Debt Avalanche** – Focus on the highest-interest debt first to minimize total cost. This saves the most money long-term, though it may take longer to see progress.

The key is commitment. Pick one method and stick with it until every toxic debt is gone.

Avoiding Future Traps

Once free, prevention is critical. Some tactics:

- Use credit cards only for expenses you already planned and can pay in full.
- Build an emergency fund so surprises don't send you back into debt.
- Delay gratification—wait, save, and buy without financing when possible.

The Emotional Freedom of Debt-Free Living

Being debt-free isn't just financial—it's emotional. Imagine receiving a paycheck and knowing every dollar is yours to spend, save, or invest. No interest payments, no late fees, no lingering stress.

Debt keeps you in survival mode. Freedom from it puts you in growth mode.

The Takeaway

Debt traps are designed to enslave. Escaping them requires discipline, strategy, and a commitment to never fall back. Credit and loans can be tools, but only if they serve your future rather than robbing it.

Growth accelerates when you stop paying for yesterday and start investing in tomorrow.

Automating Savings and Investments

Most people don't fail at saving because they lack discipline—they fail because they rely on willpower. Willpower fades. Habits slip. Life gets busy. That's why the wealthy often rely on a smarter strategy: **automation.**

By setting up systems that move money before you can spend it, you turn saving and investing from a choice into a default. This single shift can transform your finances more than any budgeting trick.

Why Automation Works

Behavioral science shows we're terrible at resisting temptation. Left unchecked, money sitting in a checking account tends to get spent. Automation removes the temptation by moving money the moment it arrives.

This is called **paying yourself first.** Instead of saving what's left over after expenses, you save immediately and spend what's left over after saving. The priority flips, and over time, so does your wealth.

Automating Savings

Start with a simple system:

- Direct deposit a portion of each paycheck into a dedicated savings account.
- Use bank rules to schedule automatic transfers weekly or monthly.
- Keep this account separate so you're less tempted to touch it.

Even $50 a week builds momentum. Over a year, that's $2,600 saved without thinking. Add interest or investment returns, and the effect compounds further.

Automating Investments

Investing can also be automated through tools like:

- **401(k) contributions** – taken directly from your paycheck, often with employer matching (free money).
- **Robo-advisors** – automatically invest deposits into diversified portfolios.
- **Recurring transfers** – set up automatic investments into index funds or brokerage accounts.

This system leverages **dollar-cost averaging**—investing the same amount regularly, regardless of market conditions. Over time, this smooths out volatility and builds wealth without emotional decision-making.

The Psychological Advantage

Automation reduces decision fatigue. Instead of wondering, *Should I save this month? Should I invest now or wait?*—the system decides for you. You bypass procrastination, fear, and inconsistency.

It also reframes identity. Once automated, you stop seeing yourself as someone who "tries to save" and start seeing yourself as someone who **always invests.** That identity shift is powerful.

Guardrails for Success

For automation to work, you need a few guardrails:

- **Emergency buffer** – build basic savings first so you don't have to pull from investments in a crisis.
- **Check quarterly** – review automated systems to ensure they align with current goals.
- **Increase gradually** – when income rises, increase automatic contributions instead of lifestyle spending.

This ensures automation remains sustainable and aligned with your bigger picture.

Real-World Example

Maria earns $4,000 monthly. She automates $400 into her retirement account, $200 into an index fund, and $100 into an emergency fund. Without lifting a finger, she saves and invests $700 a month. After five years, she has over $50,000—money she likely would have spent otherwise.

The difference wasn't discipline. It was automation.

The Takeaway

Automation is the ultimate wealth hack. It removes willpower from the equation, ensures consistency, and allows compounding to work in your favor.

Growth doesn't come from big, dramatic decisions—it comes from small, consistent actions executed automatically over time.

The Psychology of Delayed Gratification

If there's one mental habit that separates the wealthy from the struggling, it's the ability to delay gratification. This means resisting the temptation of immediate pleasure in favor of long-term rewards. It's simple in theory, but challenging in practice—because our brains are wired for "now."

Understanding and mastering this psychology is essential if you want to grow beyond short-term survival and build lasting wealth.

The Marshmallow Test and Money

In the 1970s, psychologist Walter Mischel conducted the famous "marshmallow test." Children were given one marshmallow and told they could eat it immediately or wait 15 minutes to receive two. The study followed them into adulthood. The kids who waited—those with self-control—ended up with higher incomes, better health, and greater success.

Wealth works the same way. Every time you choose to invest instead of splurge, you're passing your own marshmallow test. You're sacrificing a smaller "now" for a bigger "later."

Why Immediate Rewards Are So Tempting

Our brains evolved for survival, not long-term planning. For most of human history, resources were scarce and uncertain. If food was available, you ate it immediately. That wiring still drives us today—except now it pushes us to overspend on gadgets, clothes, or takeout.

Marketers exploit this bias with "limited-time offers," credit cards, and instant checkout buttons. They feed the desire for immediate gratification while hiding the long-term costs.

How Wealthy People Think Differently

The wealthy don't avoid pleasure—they just shift it. Instead of asking, *What feels good now?* they ask, *What will feel even better later?*

For example, instead of buying a luxury car on credit, they invest in assets first. Years later, the returns from those investments can buy the car outright—without debt, without stress, and often with wealth still growing.

This mindset creates exponential results. Small sacrifices today compound into massive freedom tomorrow.

Training Yourself to Delay Gratification

The good news is that self-control is like a muscle—you can train it. Some practical strategies:

1. **Pause purchases** – Wait 24–48 hours before buying non-essentials. Often, the urge fades.
2. **Visualize the trade-off** – Remind yourself: "If I spend $100 today, that's $1,000 less in 10 years." (Thanks to compounding, this is often true.)
3. **Automate saving first** – By removing money before you can spend it, you bypass temptation.
4. **Reward yourself strategically** – Allow small indulgences, but tie them to milestones (e.g., paying off debt, hitting savings goals). This balances discipline with enjoyment.

Delayed Gratification Beyond Money

This principle extends beyond finances. It's the same psychology behind studying instead of partying, exercising instead of lounging, or building a skill instead of scrolling endlessly. The rewards are delayed, but far greater.

Wealth is simply one visible outcome of a broader life skill: choosing tomorrow's growth over today's impulse.

The Takeaway

Mastering delayed gratification is less about deprivation and more about design. When you align your habits with long-term rewards, you create wealth, health, and freedom simultaneously.

Growth is not about saying "no" forever—it's about saying "not yet" long enough for your future self to win.

CHAPTER 5

Investing for Long-Term Riches

Stocks, ETFs, and Compounding Power

Once your foundation is solid—budgeting, saving, and eliminating bad debt—the next step is to grow your money. And in the modern world, one of the most reliable vehicles for wealth-building is the stock market. For decades, it has quietly turned ordinary people into millionaires, not through luck, but through time, patience, and the power of compounding.

Why Stocks Build Wealth

A stock is simply a piece of ownership in a company. When you buy a share of Apple or Tesla, you're not just buying a ticker symbol— you're buying a slice of the company's future earnings. As the company grows, so does your wealth.

Historically, broad stock market indexes (like the S&P 500) have returned an average of **7–10% annually** over the long run, after inflation. That may sound modest, but over decades, it snowballs into extraordinary growth.

For example, $10,000 invested in the S&P 500 in 1980 would be worth over $700,000 today. That's the magic of compounding at work.

ETFs: Investing Made Simple

Many people are intimidated by picking individual stocks. That's where **ETFs (Exchange-Traded Funds)** come in. An ETF bundles together many stocks into one investment, giving you instant diversification. Instead of betting on one company, you're buying into hundreds at once.

Think of ETFs like a basket of fruit. Instead of only buying one apple (which might rot), you buy the whole basket (so even if one fruit spoils, the others keep you nourished).

For beginners, ETFs tracking major indexes—like the S&P 500 or global markets—are often the smartest starting point. They're low-cost, diversified, and historically reliable.

The Magic of Compounding

Compounding is what makes investing powerful. It means your money earns returns, and those returns start earning returns of their own. Over time, the growth accelerates exponentially.

Here's a simple illustration:

- At 7% annual growth, $10,000 becomes $20,000 in 10 years.
- In 20 years, it grows to nearly $40,000.
- In 30 years, over $76,000.

Notice that most of the growth happens later—the "snowball effect." That's why starting early is more powerful than starting big.

Avoiding the Short-Term Trap

The biggest mistake new investors make is treating the stock market like a casino. They chase "hot stocks," panic during downturns, and try to time the market. But history shows time in the market beats timing the market.

During crashes like 2008 or 2020, many people sold in fear, locking in losses. Those who stayed invested, or even bought more, saw their portfolios recover and grow stronger.

Wealth in stocks doesn't come from prediction—it comes from patience.

A Practical Starting Plan

1. Build your emergency fund first.
2. Pay off high-interest debt.
3. Open a brokerage or retirement account.
4. Invest consistently—automate monthly contributions.
5. Stick with diversified ETFs or index funds for steady growth.

Even $200 a month invested consistently can grow into hundreds of thousands over a career.

The Takeaway

Stocks and ETFs are not about getting rich quick—they're about getting rich inevitably. When combined with compounding, consistent investing turns modest sums into lasting wealth.

Growth happens when you stop chasing quick wins and commit to the patient power of compounding.

Real Estate: When and How to Get In

Real estate has created more millionaires than almost any other asset class. It offers two powerful wealth-building features: **cash flow** and **appreciation.** But unlike buying stocks or ETFs, real estate requires careful timing, preparation, and management. Get it right, and it can transform your financial future. Get it wrong, and it can drain your savings and peace of mind.

Why Real Estate Builds Wealth

Real estate provides three main benefits:

1. **Rental income** – steady cash flow from tenants.
2. **Appreciation** – properties generally rise in value over time.
3. **Leverage** – the ability to use borrowed money (a mortgage) to control a large asset with relatively small upfront capital.

Example: You buy a $200,000 property with a $40,000 down payment. If the property rises to $250,000, your $40,000 investment has grown by $50,000—more than 100% return. That's the power of leverage.

When to Get In

Timing matters. Many people rush into real estate without being financially prepared. A good rule of thumb:

- **Emergency fund first** – Real estate is unpredictable. Vacancies, repairs, or job loss can strain your finances.
- **Stable income** – Lenders want to see reliable earnings before granting favorable mortgages.
- **Manageable debt** – If you're buried in credit card debt, real estate is not your next step.
- **Local market knowledge** – Buying blindly in a "hot" market often leads to overpaying. Research rental demand, job growth, and neighborhood trends.

Real estate is best entered once your financial foundation is solid and you're ready for long-term commitment.

How to Start Small

You don't need millions to begin. Options include:

- **House hacking** – Live in one unit of a multi-family property and rent out the others to cover the mortgage.
- **Short-term rentals** – Renting a spare room or property on platforms like Airbnb.
- **REITs (Real Estate Investment Trusts)** – Publicly traded companies that own income-generating properties. This allows you to invest in real estate without owning property directly.

Starting small reduces risk while letting you learn the ropes.

Common Pitfalls to Avoid

1. **Underestimating costs** – Repairs, taxes, insurance, and vacancies add up. Always budget beyond the mortgage.
2. **Overleveraging** – Borrowing too much can backfire if the market dips or tenants default.
3. **Ignoring cash flow** – Don't buy just for appreciation. A property that loses money monthly is not an investment—it's a liability.

Smart investors focus on positive cash flow first; appreciation is the bonus.

Real Estate as a Long Game

Property isn't a quick flip for most investors—it's a marathon. Markets rise and fall, but over decades, real estate tends to grow in value while producing steady income. That combination makes it one of the most stable wealth builders available.

The Takeaway

Real estate can be a powerful wealth vehicle—but only when entered with preparation, patience, and strategy. Start small, focus on cash flow, and avoid overleveraging.

Growth in real estate doesn't come from rushing into the market. It comes from building a strong foundation, then letting time and leverage work in your favor.

Business Ownership and Equity Wealth

If salaries and savings build stability, business ownership builds **wealth at scale.** The world's wealthiest individuals—from Elon Musk to Oprah Winfrey—didn't just earn high incomes; they owned equity in businesses. Ownership, not labor, is what creates disproportionate wealth.

Why Equity Beats Salary

A salary pays you for your time. Equity pays you for the value you create—and that value can grow infinitely.

Example: Imagine you work at a coffee shop earning $20 an hour. You can only work so many hours. Now imagine you own the coffee shop. Each barista, each customer, each sale contributes to your wealth, even if you're not physically there. The difference is leverage: ownership multiplies your efforts through people, systems, and assets.

Small Business, Big Impact

You don't need to own a multinational company to benefit. Small businesses—local shops, service companies, online brands—can provide significant wealth when managed well.

Take Sarah, who starts a home cleaning business. At first, she cleans houses herself, earning active income. Over time, she hires employees, builds a client base, and steps back from daily work. The business now runs with or without her, providing both income and equity value she could one day sell.

This shift from worker to owner is the essence of equity wealth.

Startups and High Growth

For those willing to take more risk, startups offer extraordinary upside. By owning equity in a fast-growing company—whether your own or through early-stage investment—you capture exponential value.

Think of employees who accepted stock options at companies like Amazon or Airbnb. Many became millionaires not from their salaries, but from owning even a small slice of equity.

Of course, startups carry high risk. Most fail. But the principle remains: ownership carries far greater wealth potential than wages.

Online Businesses: The Modern Gateway

The digital age has lowered barriers to business ownership. With little capital, you can start an e-commerce brand, subscription service, or content-based company from your laptop. Unlike traditional businesses, online ventures scale globally with minimal overhead.

Owning digital products—courses, apps, memberships—creates equity that produces ongoing income and can be sold later. It's business ownership in its most accessible form.

Thinking Like an Owner

Even if you're currently an employee, you can adopt an ownership mindset. Ask yourself:

- Can I negotiate stock options instead of only salary?
- Can I start a side business that grows into full ownership?
- Can I invest in other people's businesses (equity crowdfunding, private deals)?

Every step toward equity shifts you from trading time to multiplying wealth.

The Takeaway

Salaries pay the bills. Ownership builds empires. Equity—whether in small businesses, startups, or digital ventures—is the true driver of long-term wealth.

Growth comes when you stop asking, *How can I earn more per hour?* and start asking, *How can I own something that grows while I sleep?*

Risk vs. Reward: Balancing Short-Term vs. Long-Term

Every investment decision involves a trade-off between risk and reward. Play it too safe, and your money barely grows. Take on too much risk, and you may lose it all. Wealth isn't built by avoiding risk—it's built by **managing it wisely.**

Understanding how to balance short-term safety with long-term growth is what separates successful investors from gamblers.

The Spectrum of Risk

Think of risk as a spectrum:

- **Low risk**: savings accounts, government bonds. Safe but with tiny returns.
- **Moderate risk**: index funds, diversified ETFs, rental properties. Balanced growth with manageable volatility.
- **High risk**: individual stocks, startups, crypto, speculative real estate. Potential for massive reward—or massive loss.

The right mix depends on your goals, timeline, and risk tolerance.

The Cost of Playing Too Safe

Many people keep all their money in savings accounts "just in case." The problem is inflation. If inflation averages 3% and your savings earn 1%, your money loses value every year. Safety becomes silent loss.

Example: $10,000 left in a savings account earning 1% will be worth only about $7,400 in purchasing power after 20 years. Playing too safe means falling behind.

The Danger of Chasing Quick Wins

On the other side, chasing hot trends—like speculative stocks or cryptocurrencies—can feel exciting but often ends in losses. Most people jump in too late, after prices have already soared, and panic-sell when they drop.

Wealthy investors don't gamble. They take calculated risks aligned with their long-term vision.

The Time Horizon Advantage

The longer your time horizon, the more risk you can safely take. Why? Because markets are volatile short-term but trend upward long-term.

For example, the stock market has had many one-year losses, but over any 20-year period in history, it has always delivered positive returns. This means a 25-year-old can invest aggressively in stocks, while a 65-year-old approaching retirement may shift toward safer assets.

Diversification: The Safety Net

The golden rule of risk management is diversification—spreading money across asset classes so no single failure wipes you out.

- Stocks provide growth.
- Bonds provide stability.
- Real estate provides income and appreciation.
- Cash provides liquidity.

Together, they create resilience. You don't need to predict the future if you're diversified.

Emotional Risk Management

Risk isn't just numbers—it's psychology. Many people overestimate their risk tolerance until a market crash hits. They panic, sell at the bottom, and lock in losses.

The solution is building a portfolio you can emotionally handle. If you can't sleep when markets drop 20%, you're too exposed. Long-term investing only works if you can stay the course.

The Takeaway

Risk is not the enemy—recklessness is. Avoiding risk keeps you poor. Chasing risk blindly keeps you broke. Managing risk strategically builds wealth.

Growth comes when you balance today's stability with tomorrow's opportunity—protecting your present while multiplying your future.

CHAPTER 6

Leveraging Opportunities in the New Economy

AI and Digital Tools That Build Wealth Faster

In the past, building wealth often meant long hours, physical labor, and limited opportunities. Today, technology has rewritten the rules. Artificial Intelligence (AI) and digital tools are creating shortcuts that allow individuals to earn, scale, and invest faster than ever before. The new economy rewards those who know how to leverage these tools—not those who ignore them.

Why Technology Is the New Leverage

Wealth is built through leverage—multiplying your effort without multiplying your time. Historically, leverage came from capital (money working for you) or labor (hiring others to work for you). Today, digital leverage is even more powerful: tools and algorithms that can scale your impact globally, often at little cost.

A single entrepreneur with AI-powered tools can now compete with large companies. This is not the future—it's happening right now.

AI as Your Personal Assistant

AI is already transforming how individuals earn:

- **Content creation** – AI tools write, edit, and generate graphics in minutes.
- **Marketing automation** – Personalized ads and emails can run 24/7 with minimal input.
- **Financial planning** – Robo-advisors optimize investments at a fraction of traditional costs.
- **Productivity** – Virtual assistants automate scheduling, research, and even customer support.

Instead of replacing you, AI extends you—allowing you to produce more in less time. The competitive edge goes to those who embrace it.

Digital Tools That Multiply Earnings

Beyond AI, countless platforms lower barriers to wealth-building:

- **E-commerce platforms** (Shopify, Amazon) let you sell globally.
- **Creator platforms** (YouTube, Substack, TikTok) monetize your audience.
- **Freelance platforms** (Upwork, Fiverr) connect you instantly to global clients.
- **Investment apps** (Robinhood, Vanguard, Coinbase) make wealth-building accessible with a few taps.

These tools democratize opportunity. What once required capital, offices, and networks can now be started with a laptop and internet connection.

The Speed Advantage

The biggest benefit of AI and digital tools is **speed.** What used to take months can now be done in days or hours. Launching a website, testing a product idea, or reaching thousands of potential customers no longer requires teams or big budgets.

Speed matters because it lets you experiment more often. Failures become cheaper, and successes scale faster.

Avoiding the Shiny Object Trap

With endless tools available, the danger is distraction. Many people waste time chasing the latest platform instead of mastering a few that actually move the needle. The wealthy don't chase tools—they select strategically, automate essentials, and stay focused on outcomes.

A Practical Roadmap

1. **Choose one wealth path** (content, e-commerce, freelancing, or investing).
2. **Pick two to three tools** that amplify that path.
3. **Automate repetitive tasks** so you can focus on high-value work.
4. **Reinvest time saved** into learning, scaling, or building new streams.

This way, tools serve you, rather than overwhelm you.

The Takeaway

AI and digital tools don't just make life convenient—they're accelerators of wealth. Those who adopt them gain leverage, speed, and reach. Those who ignore them risk being left behind.

Growth in the new economy is no longer about working harder—it's about working smarter with the right digital allies.

Global Freelancing and Remote Work Opportunities

Work is no longer tied to geography. Thanks to the internet, companies and individuals can hire talent from anywhere, and skilled workers can serve clients worldwide without leaving home. This global shift has unlocked new opportunities to earn, diversify income, and escape the limitations of local job markets.

For those willing to adapt, freelancing and remote work can be powerful stepping stones to financial independence.

Why the Shift Matters

In the old economy, your income depended on your local economy. A graphic designer in a small town might struggle to find clients, while the same designer in New York could charge premium rates. Today, platforms like Upwork, Fiverr, and Toptal connect that small-town designer to global demand.

Remote work also benefits employees. Companies are increasingly open to hiring across borders, offering competitive salaries without requiring relocation. For workers, this means access to higher-paying markets without higher living costs.

Freelancing: Freedom and Flexibility

Freelancing allows you to sell skills directly—writing, design, programming, marketing, consulting—without traditional employment. The advantages are clear:

- **Flexibility** – You choose your clients, schedule, and projects.
- **Scalability** – Start part-time alongside a job, then scale as demand grows.
- **Global reach** – Earn in stronger currencies while living in lower-cost regions.

Example: A software developer in India earning $1,500 locally can earn $5,000 or more monthly serving U.S. or European clients remotely. That gap in opportunity is life-changing.

Remote Work: Stability Meets Freedom

While freelancing offers flexibility, remote jobs provide **stability**— steady paychecks, benefits, and career growth, but without commuting or geographic limits.

Roles in tech, marketing, finance, customer support, and education are increasingly remote-friendly. For many, this hybrid path—stable remote employment plus side freelancing—creates the perfect balance of security and growth.

Building a Global Career

To thrive in this new economy, you must:

1. **Package your skills** – Learn how to present yourself online through portfolios, profiles, and clear value propositions.
2. **Upskill continuously** – Stay relevant by mastering in-demand digital tools and platforms.
3. **Manage yourself** – Remote work requires discipline, communication skills, and self-management to replace the structure of an office.

Those who treat freelancing or remote work casually often struggle. Those who treat it like a business or career flourish.

Risks and Rewards

Global freelancing isn't perfect. Competition is intense, especially for low-skill tasks, and some clients undervalue remote workers. But the solution isn't avoiding it—it's **differentiating yourself.** Specializing, niching down, and building a strong reputation are the antidotes to commoditization.

The Takeaway

The future of work is borderless. Whether through freelancing platforms or remote employment, the ability to earn globally is no longer reserved for a few—it's available to anyone with skills and internet access.

Growth comes when you stop limiting your income to your zip code and start seeing the world as your marketplace.

Turning Knowledge into Products: Books, Courses, Apps

In the old economy, wealth was tied to physical products—factories, machinery, and inventory. In the new economy, wealth often comes from **knowledge products**—digital creations that can be built once and sold infinitely. Books, courses, and apps are modern assets: they require upfront effort but can generate ongoing income for years.

The shift is profound: your brain can be your most valuable factory.

Why Knowledge Is a Scalable Asset

When you sell your time, you can only serve one client or employer at a time. When you package your knowledge, you can serve thousands—or millions—simultaneously.

Example: A teacher can instruct 30 students in a classroom. But if that teacher creates an online course, they can teach 30,000 students worldwide, often at a fraction of the cost per student. The work is done once, the rewards repeat.

This is scalability—the essence of wealth in the digital age.

Books: Authority and Residual Income

Writing a book no longer requires approval from publishers. Self-publishing platforms allow anyone to share expertise globally. While royalties per copy may be modest, books build credibility and open doors to speaking, consulting, and brand partnerships.

Even niche books—like guides to coding, fitness programs, or language learning—can provide a steady trickle of royalties that add up over time.

Courses: Teaching at Scale

Online courses are one of the fastest-growing industries. Platforms like Udemy, Teachable, and Skillshare allow anyone to turn skills into structured lessons.

A designer can teach logo creation. A lawyer can teach contract basics. A musician can teach guitar online. Unlike one-on-one teaching, a course scales infinitely—students can enroll while you sleep.

Successful courses don't just share knowledge; they solve problems. The more practical and results-driven, the higher the value.

Apps: Digital Tools as Products

Apps and software solve problems at scale. While more technical, no-code platforms now allow non-programmers to create apps without deep coding skills. A simple budgeting tool, workout tracker, or productivity app can reach global users.

The key is focusing on utility. You don't need the next Facebook—you need something that solves a clear, specific problem for a defined group of people.

The Long Game of Knowledge Products

Knowledge products often grow slowly. A course may sell only a handful of copies at first. A book may sit unnoticed. An app may attract only early users. But over time, if the product solves real problems, word of mouth and digital marketing amplify growth.

Unlike freelancing, where income stops if you stop working, knowledge products keep selling long after the work is done. That makes them **digital assets**—a cornerstone of passive income.

The Takeaway

Your skills and knowledge are not just tools to trade for hours—they can be packaged into products that scale without limit. Books, courses, and apps turn expertise into equity.

Growth comes when you stop only selling your time and start selling what you know.

Investing in Yourself: Skills That Guarantee Higher Income

The most valuable investment you will ever make is not in stocks, real estate, or businesses—it's in **yourself.** Assets can rise and fall, but your skills, mindset, and knowledge are portable, compounding, and inflation-proof. They travel with you, adapt to any economy, and unlock opportunities no market crash can take away.

Why Self-Investment Outperforms

Consider this: If you invest $1,000 in the stock market, you might earn 7–10% annually. If you invest the same $1,000 in a new skill— say coding, sales, or design—you could increase your income by thousands per year, every year, for decades. That's a return no traditional asset can match.

This is why the wealthy obsess over learning. They know that personal growth multiplies financial growth.

Skills That Always Pay Off

Certain skills consistently lead to higher income across industries and generations:

- **Communication** – Public speaking, persuasive writing, and negotiation increase influence and earning potential.

- **Sales and marketing** – The ability to sell—products, services, or ideas—is the engine of business and career growth.
- **Technology literacy** – Coding, data analysis, AI tools, and digital platforms are the language of the new economy.
- **Financial literacy** – Understanding money management, investing, and risk ensures wealth isn't just earned but kept.
- **Leadership** – The ability to manage people, solve problems, and inspire teams multiplies your impact.

These are "evergreen" skills—relevant in any economy, adaptable across careers.

The Compound Effect of Learning

Self-investment compounds like money does. A single skill learned today creates opportunities tomorrow, which open doors to further growth.

Example: A freelancer who learns copywriting can charge more. If they also learn digital marketing, they can offer bundled services. Later, if they learn leadership, they can hire a team and scale into an agency. Each skill compounds the value of the last.

How to Invest in Yourself Practically

1. **Books and courses** – Affordable, high-return ways to acquire knowledge.
2. **Mentorship** – Learning directly from those ahead of you shortcuts years of trial and error.
3. **Communities** – Surround yourself with ambitious peers; environment shapes mindset.
4. **Experiments** – Side projects and small ventures provide hands-on learning faster than theory.

The key is not just consuming knowledge, but applying it. A skill only compounds when put into practice.

Avoiding the Trap of Passive Learning

Many people mistake watching videos or reading books for progress. But passive learning without action creates an illusion of growth. True investment requires application: building, testing, failing, and adjusting.

Wealth doesn't come from what you know—it comes from what you **do** with what you know.

The Takeaway

Every dollar and hour you put into yourself creates exponential returns over your lifetime. Markets can crash, companies can fold, but skills compound forever.

Growth begins with self-investment. When you become more valuable, every opportunity—job, business, or investment—expands with you.

CHAPTER 7

Protecting and Growing Your Wealth

Taxes and Smart Financial Planning

Making money is only half the game—keeping it is the other. For many, taxes are their single largest expense, often bigger than rent, food, or investments combined. Yet while most people grumble about taxes, the wealthy study them. They don't evade taxes illegally; they minimize them legally through **strategy and planning.**

Financial freedom isn't just about how much you earn—it's about how much you keep.

Why Taxes Matter So Much

Imagine two people, both earning $100,000 a year.

- Person A pays 30% in taxes and keeps $70,000.
- Person B uses legal strategies to reduce their tax burden to 20% and keeps $80,000.

Over 20 years, that difference adds up to $200,000—without either earning a dollar more. Smart planning doesn't just save money; it accelerates wealth.

How the Wealthy Think About Taxes

The wealthy see taxes as a system to be understood, not feared. They structure their lives around tax efficiency:

- **Business ownership** – Many expenses become deductible when tied to income generation.
- **Investments** – Long-term capital gains are often taxed lower than salary income.
- **Retirement accounts** – Tools like 401(k)s, IRAs, or equivalents worldwide defer or reduce taxes.
- **Real estate** – Depreciation and deductions often reduce taxable income even while cash flow is positive.

They play the long game: minimizing taxable income today while building assets that grow tomorrow.

The Power of Financial Planning

Taxes are just one part of the bigger picture. Smart financial planning connects taxes, savings, investments, insurance, and estate planning into one strategy.

Without a plan, money leaks through poor decisions—penalties, missed deductions, unnecessary fees. With a plan, every dollar has a role: earning, protecting, or compounding wealth.

Practical Steps to Smarter Taxes

1. **Track everything** – Keep records of income, expenses, and receipts. Organization unlocks deductions.
2. **Use tax-advantaged accounts** – Contribute to retirement or investment accounts that reduce taxable income.
3. **Separate business and personal expenses** – If you run a side hustle or business, clean bookkeeping prevents mistakes and maximizes write-offs.
4. **Consult professionals** – A good accountant often saves more in taxes than they cost in fees.

A Common Mistake: Waiting Too Long

Many people only think about taxes in April (or at filing season in their country). By then, it's too late to change much. The wealthy plan year-round—adjusting investments, contributions, and expenses proactively.

The Takeaway

Taxes are not a punishment—they're part of the game. But like any game, those who know the rules win more often. By combining tax strategies with overall financial planning, you keep more of what you earn and build wealth faster.

Growth doesn't just come from earning—it comes from protecting. And one of the most powerful shields you have is smart tax planning.

Insurance: Protecting What You've Built

Building wealth takes years of effort, but losing it can happen in a single moment. A medical emergency, car accident, natural disaster, or unexpected death can wipe out savings and derail financial progress. That's why the wealthy don't see insurance as a cost—they see it as **protection.**

If assets are the bricks of wealth, insurance is the guardrail that keeps them from collapsing.

Why Insurance Matters

Without insurance, you're gambling with your financial future. One lawsuit or hospital bill can undo years of disciplined saving and investing. With insurance, those risks shift from you to an institution that can absorb them.

It's not glamorous. You won't brag about your policy at dinner parties. But insurance ensures your wealth-building journey doesn't get derailed by a single unpredictable event.

The Core Types Everyone Needs

1. **Health Insurance** – Medical bills are one of the leading causes of bankruptcy worldwide. Even a short hospital stay can cost more than most families have saved. Health coverage is non-negotiable.
2. **Life Insurance** – If others depend on your income, life insurance ensures they're protected if something happens to

you. Term life is often the best value—affordable and straightforward.

3. **Disability Insurance** – Your ability to earn is your biggest asset. If illness or injury prevents you from working, disability coverage keeps income flowing.
4. **Property Insurance** – Homeowners or renters insurance protects against theft, fire, and natural disasters.
5. **Liability Insurance** – Accidents happen. Liability coverage shields you from lawsuits that could otherwise strip away savings and assets.

Avoiding Over-Insurance

While insurance is essential, not all policies are worth buying. Many products are designed more to enrich insurers than protect you—like expensive whole life insurance, extended warranties, or redundant coverage.

The rule: Cover catastrophic risks (those that would ruin you financially), not minor inconveniences. Insure what you can't afford to lose. Self-insure the rest by using your emergency fund.

The Wealthy Approach to Insurance

Wealthy individuals often layer coverage strategically. For example, they may hold umbrella liability insurance—a relatively low-cost policy that provides millions in extra coverage above home and auto insurance. This small investment protects their larger portfolio from lawsuits.

They don't view insurance as wasted money. They see it as the cost of security—the foundation that allows them to take bigger risks elsewhere (like investing or business) without fear of being wiped out.

The Peace of Mind Dividend

Beyond the numbers, insurance buys something priceless: peace of mind. Knowing that your family, health, and assets are protected frees mental energy. That energy can then be redirected into growth instead of worry.

The Takeaway

Insurance doesn't grow wealth—it protects it. Without it, you risk losing everything to one unpredictable event. With it, you create a safety net strong enough to support long-term growth.

Growth is not only about building—it's about protecting what you've built so it lasts.

Avoiding Scams and "Get Rich Quick" Traps

For as long as people have wanted wealth, others have tried to exploit that desire. Scams and "get rich quick" schemes prey on impatience, greed, and ignorance. They promise shortcuts but usually deliver losses. Protecting your wealth means learning to recognize and avoid these traps before they cost you money—or worse, your trust in investing altogether.

Why We Fall for Traps

Scams succeed because they appeal to human psychology. They offer:

- **Speed** – "Make $10,000 in 30 days."
- **Simplicity** – "Just follow three steps."
- **Exclusivity** – "Secret strategies the rich don't want you to know."

In uncertain times, people crave certainty. Scammers package hope and disguise it as opportunity. Recognizing the emotional pull is the first defense.

Classic Red Flags

1. **Guaranteed high returns** – No legitimate investment guarantees outsized profits with zero risk. If it sounds too good to be true, it is.
2. **Pressure to act fast** – Scammers push urgency so you don't have time to think or research.
3. **Lack of transparency** – If you don't understand how the money is made, or if details are vague, walk away.
4. **Celebrity or influencer hype** – Endorsements don't equal legitimacy. Scams often "borrow" authority figures to build false trust.

The Cost of Falling for Shortcuts

Beyond losing money, scams create something more damaging: cynicism. Victims often swear off investing entirely, believing "the system is rigged." This mindset keeps them stuck while others grow.

Real wealth requires patience and discipline. There are no shortcuts. The only "secret" is consistency applied over years.

Modern Variations of Old Tricks

- **Crypto pump-and-dumps** – Inflated hype followed by collapse.
- **Fake gurus** – Selling expensive courses that teach little beyond motivation.
- **Ponzi schemes** – Paying old investors with new investors' money until the scheme collapses.
- **High-risk trading apps** – Gamified platforms that encourage reckless bets disguised as investing.

The scams evolve, but the patterns stay the same: promises of fast, easy money.

Building Scam Immunity

1. **Educate yourself** – Financial literacy is the best defense. The more you understand money, the harder it is to fool you.
2. **Slow down** – If pressured to act immediately, that's a signal to pause. Real opportunities don't expire overnight.
3. **Ask: Who benefits?** – If someone profits more from selling you the idea than from the idea itself, be skeptical.
4. **Stick to fundamentals** – Proven strategies—budgeting, saving, investing in assets—always outperform shortcuts.

The Takeaway

Scams and shortcuts are not just financial traps—they're mindset traps. They distract you from the steady, proven path of real wealth creation.

Growth comes when you reject illusions of easy money and commit to the long game. The slow path is not only safer—it's the only path that lasts.

Continuous Reinvestment: Making Your Money Work Harder

The wealthy don't just earn money—they put it to work, again and again. This is the principle of **continuous reinvestment.** Instead of cashing out profits and inflating their lifestyle, they recycle earnings into new opportunities that compound wealth over time.

Money, when treated as an employee, should never sit idle. It should always be working somewhere—earning interest, generating dividends, or creating new income streams.

Why Reinvestment Multiplies Wealth

Imagine planting an apple tree. In a few years, it produces fruit. You could eat all the apples now, or you could replant some seeds. Over time, you don't just have one tree—you have an orchard. That's reinvestment in action.

The same applies to money. When you reinvest profits instead of spending them, each cycle produces more income, which can then be reinvested again. This is how ordinary investments snowball into extraordinary fortunes.

Examples of Continuous Reinvestment

- **Dividends** – Instead of pocketing dividend payouts from stocks, reinvest them to buy more shares. Over decades, this dramatically boosts portfolio growth.
- **Rental income** – Use profits from one property to fund the down payment for another.
- **Business profits** – Channel earnings back into marketing, product development, or hiring—scaling income rather than extracting it too early.
- **Side hustles** – Reinvest initial profits into tools, automation, or outsourcing to grow capacity.

The pattern is clear: money makes more money when you keep it in motion.

The Danger of Stagnation

Many people sabotage growth by cashing out too soon. They spend investment returns on vacations, cars, or upgrades, leaving their "apple tree" too small to sustain future needs.

This doesn't mean you should never enjoy your money—it means striking balance. Spend some, but reinvest consistently so your wealth continues to grow.

Long-Term vs. Short-Term Thinking

The reinvestment mindset requires patience. In the short term, you may feel like you're missing out compared to peers who spend freely. But in the long term, the difference is dramatic.

Example: Two investors each earn $5,000 in stock dividends annually. One spends it; the other reinvests. After 20 years at a 7% return, the spender still has $5,000 yearly. The reinvestor has over $200,000 more in wealth and $20,000 yearly dividends.

The lesson? Reinvestment creates exponential rewards that spending can never match.

Practical Ways to Apply It

1. Automate dividend reinvestment plans (DRIPs).
2. Allocate a fixed percentage of business profits back into growth.
3. Set rules: for every $1,000 earned in passive income, reinvest at least $700.
4. Treat reinvestment as a non-negotiable habit, just like saving.

The Takeaway

Wealth isn't built by earning once—it's built by reinvesting continuously. Every dollar you put back into assets, instead of consumption, multiplies your future freedom.

Growth happens when you resist the urge to harvest too early and instead let your orchard of assets grow.

CHAPTER 8

The Road to Financial Freedom

Setting Milestones: $10k, $100k, $1M Net Worth

Financial freedom is not achieved in a single leap—it's built step by step. Like climbing a mountain, you don't start at the summit. You set milestones along the way, each one proof of progress and motivation to keep going.

Clear milestones transform wealth-building from an abstract dream into a measurable journey. They give you checkpoints, small victories that make the long road tangible.

The First $10,000: Building Discipline

The first milestone is not about the amount—it's about the habit. Saving your first $10,000 teaches discipline, budgeting, and delayed gratification. It forces you to take control of spending and build consistency.

At this stage, every dollar matters. Cutting small expenses, automating savings, and avoiding debt lay the foundation. Many underestimate this milestone, but once you cross it, momentum builds. You prove to yourself: *I can save. I can grow.*

The First $100,000: The Wealth Accelerator

Investor Charlie Munger once said, *"The first $100,000 is a bitch, but you gotta do it."* Why? Because it's the hardest—and the most important.

At $100,000, compounding starts to work noticeably. A 7% return turns into $7,000 per year, without you lifting a finger. That's more than most side hustles pay. From here, wealth grows faster—not just from what you add, but from what your money adds.

Reaching this milestone requires more than just saving—it demands **earning more, spending wisely, and investing consistently.** It's the bridge from financial stability to true wealth-building.

The First $1,000,000: Freedom in Sight

The seven-figure mark carries psychological weight. It's the point where money can generate enough income to cover many lifestyles without constant labor. A $1 million portfolio earning 6% annually produces $60,000 a year—enough for financial independence in many regions.

But reaching this milestone doesn't happen by accident. It requires years of consistency, reinvestment, and avoiding big mistakes (like excessive debt or panic-selling investments). By this point, systems, not effort, drive growth.

Why Milestones Matter

Without milestones, wealth feels endless—like chasing the horizon. With them, you break the journey into achievable steps. Each milestone reinforces discipline, provides motivation, and gives you permission to celebrate progress.

Think of it like fitness: running a marathon is daunting, but reaching each mile marker keeps you moving. Wealth works the same way.

The Takeaway

Wealth is not built overnight—it's built milestone by milestone. The first $10k proves you can save. The first $100k proves compounding works. The first $1M proves financial freedom is within reach.

Growth is not about rushing to the summit—it's about honoring each checkpoint along the climb.

Designing Your Rich Life: Freedom, Choices, Legacy

Reaching financial milestones is important, but money alone doesn't define a rich life. Many people accumulate wealth only to feel empty, trapped, or directionless. That's because they never stopped to ask: *What am I building this for?*

Designing your rich life means aligning money with meaning. It's about using wealth as a tool to create freedom, expand choices, and leave a legacy that outlives you.

Freedom: The Ultimate Currency

At its core, money buys one thing most of all: **time.** When you're financially free, you're no longer forced to trade every hour for income. You can choose how you spend your days—working, creating, traveling, or resting.

Freedom is deeply personal. For one person, it might mean early retirement. For another, the ability to take summers off. For another still, simply paying bills without stress. The point is not a universal definition, but a personal one.

A rich life is not necessarily about more possessions—it's about more **control.**

Choices: Expanding Possibility

Wealth expands options. Without it, you're stuck saying yes to whatever pays the bills. With it, you can say no to toxic jobs, yes to meaningful work, or yes to adventures you once thought impossible.

Think of choices like doors. Poverty leaves most doors closed. Wealth gradually opens them. The more doors open, the more fully you can design life on your terms.

Example: Two parents both earn enough to live comfortably. One designs their rich life to include flexibility—choosing a remote job and modest home so they can spend more time with children. The other prioritizes luxury travel and fine dining. Both are valid—because both reflect conscious choice.

Legacy: Beyond Yourself

True wealth extends beyond personal comfort—it creates impact. Legacy is about what you leave behind: not just assets, but values, memories, and opportunities for others.

Legacy could mean funding your children's education, supporting causes you care about, or building businesses that employ others. It could mean writing a book that inspires future generations, or simply being remembered as someone who lived with purpose.

The wealthy think generationally. They don't just ask, *How will this money serve me?* They ask, *How will it serve those after me?*

Avoiding the Empty Rich Life

Too many people chase someone else's version of "rich"—the cars, the house, the status symbols—only to discover they don't feel fulfilled. Designing your rich life prevents this trap by grounding wealth in your own values.

A practical exercise: Write down your top five values (family, freedom, contribution, creativity, adventure, etc.). Then describe how each value would show up in your ideal financial life. This creates a blueprint for a rich life that actually feels rich.

The Takeaway

Designing your rich life is about intention. Money without meaning is empty. But money aligned with freedom, choices, and legacy becomes a powerful tool for fulfillment.

Growth isn't just about building wealth—it's about designing the life that wealth makes possible.

Building Systems That Run Without You

Financial freedom doesn't come from working harder—it comes from building systems that keep running whether you're there or not. These systems generate income, manage expenses, and grow wealth automatically, freeing you from the constant cycle of effort.

The wealthy understand this deeply: they don't just build businesses, investments, or habits—they build **systems.**

Why Systems Beat Effort

Effort is linear: one hour of work equals one hour of pay. Systems are exponential: a process, investment, or automation continues to produce results on its own.

Think of vending machines. A person stocking them once a week earns from dozens of daily sales without being present. Now scale that idea into investments, online businesses, or automated finances, and you see why systems create lasting wealth.

Systems in Money Management

Your personal finances can—and should—be systemized. Examples:

- **Automated transfers** that move money into savings or investments.
- **Bill pay automation** that eliminates late fees.
- **Budgeting apps** that categorize spending in real time.

These systems reduce errors, save time, and enforce discipline without willpower.

Systems in Business

Entrepreneurs often get stuck because their business depends entirely on them. If they stop working, income stops. The shift to wealth happens when systems replace constant involvement:

- Hiring employees or contractors.
- Automating sales, customer support, or marketing.
- Creating standard operating procedures that let others run operations.

A business with strong systems is not just income—it's an asset that can be scaled or sold.

Systems in Investing

Wealthy investors don't check markets daily. They set up automated contributions, diversified portfolios, and rebalancing rules. The system manages growth while they focus on bigger opportunities.

This protects them from emotional decision-making—the biggest killer of investment returns.

The Freedom Multiplier

When systems run without you, your time is freed for higher-value pursuits—starting new ventures, building relationships, or simply living. Systems don't just grow wealth; they multiply freedom.

Example: Emma creates an online course. She automates sales with email funnels and hires a virtual assistant to handle support. Within a year, the system generates $5,000 a month with only a few hours of oversight. That's the difference between a hustle and a system.

The Takeaway

Wealth is not about doing everything yourself—it's about designing systems that do the work for you. From personal finance to business to investing, systems create consistency, scale, and freedom.

Growth happens when you stop being the engine and start being the architect of systems that run without you.

Staying Adaptable: How the Wealthy Keep Getting Richer

The world changes fast. Industries rise and fall, technologies disrupt entire markets, and financial strategies that worked yesterday may not work tomorrow. The wealthy don't avoid change—they anticipate and adapt to it. That adaptability is why their wealth not only survives but multiplies.

If you want to stay financially free, adaptability must become one of your strongest assets.

Why Adaptability Is Wealth's Silent Driver

Most people resist change. They cling to what's familiar, even when it stops working. But wealth is built by those who notice shifts early and adjust their strategies.

- Farmers who embraced machinery outproduced those who resisted.
- Businesses that moved online thrived while physical-only shops struggled.
- Investors who recognized digital trends (like cloud computing or AI) captured gains others ignored.

The pattern is clear: adaptability protects you from obsolescence and positions you for growth.

The Wealthy Stay Students

The wealthy rarely assume they know everything. Instead, they stay curious. They read, network, attend conferences, and hire experts. They're not afraid to question old assumptions or pivot when new opportunities arise.

This humility keeps them relevant. While others dismiss new ideas as "fads," the wealthy test and learn—adopting what works, discarding what doesn't.

Diversification as Adaptability

Adaptability also shows up in how wealth is managed. The wealthy don't keep all assets in one basket. They diversify across industries, geographies, and asset classes. This means when one area declines, others thrive.

For example, if real estate slows, their stock portfolio or digital ventures keep growing. Diversification is adaptability in action.

Emotional Flexibility

Adaptability isn't just financial—it's emotional. Markets crash, businesses fail, and industries collapse. Many people panic and quit. The wealthy see setbacks as signals to adjust, not stop.

They ask: *What is this teaching me? How can I reposition?* This mindset turns crises into catalysts for reinvention.

Practical Ways to Build Adaptability

1. **Keep learning** – Dedicate time each week to books, podcasts, or mentors.
2. **Test small** – Experiment with new tools, platforms, or investments on a small scale before committing fully.

3. **Review regularly** – Quarterly or annually, audit your finances, habits, and goals. Adjust to current realities.
4. **Stay liquid** – Keep part of your portfolio in accessible assets so you can move quickly when opportunities appear.

The Wealth Compounding Effect

Because the wealthy adapt, they're always positioned for the next wave of growth. Each cycle—whether in technology, markets, or industries—creates new wealth for those prepared. While others cling to the past, they ride the future.

The Takeaway

Staying rich isn't about finding one formula and freezing it—it's about staying flexible, curious, and ready to pivot. Adaptability is the engine that allows wealth to survive uncertainty and thrive in change.

Growth is not about avoiding change—it's about embracing it as the path to greater freedom.

Glossary of Wealth-Building Terms

401(k)

A U.S. retirement savings plan offered by employers, allowing employees to contribute pre-tax income and often receive employer matching contributions.

Abundance Mindset

The belief that opportunities and wealth are not limited, encouraging growth, generosity, and long-term thinking. Opposite of scarcity mindset.

Active Income

Money earned by directly trading time or skills for payment—such as salaries, hourly wages, freelancing, or side hustles.

Asset

Anything that puts money in your pocket or increases in value over time (e.g., stocks, rental property, intellectual property).

Automation

Using systems, tools, or technology to manage money or business tasks without constant manual effort (e.g., automatic savings transfers, marketing funnels).

Budget

A spending plan that assigns income toward essentials, wants, and savings/investments, ensuring money is directed with purpose.

Cash Flow

The movement of money in and out of your accounts. Positive cash flow means more money is coming in than going out.

Compound Interest

The process of earning returns on both your original investment and the returns it generates, creating exponential growth over time.

Continuous Reinvestment

Recycling profits or returns back into assets, businesses, or investments to accelerate long-term growth.

Credit Card Debt

High-interest debt created by carrying unpaid balances on credit cards. Often considered a "debt trap" due to compounding interest rates.

Debt Avalanche

A repayment strategy focused on paying off debts with the highest interest rate first, saving the most money long-term.

Debt Snowball

A repayment strategy focused on paying off the smallest debt balances first to build momentum and motivation.

Delayed Gratification

The ability to resist short-term pleasures in order to achieve greater long-term rewards. A key psychological driver of wealth.

Diversification

Spreading investments across different assets (stocks, bonds, real estate, etc.) to reduce risk.

Dividend

A portion of a company's profits distributed to shareholders. Often reinvested to build wealth over time.

Dollar-Cost Averaging

An investing strategy of putting in a fixed amount of money at regular intervals, regardless of market conditions, to smooth out risk.

Emergency Fund

Cash savings (usually 3–6 months of expenses) set aside for unexpected events like job loss, medical bills, or car repairs.

Equity

Ownership in a business or asset. Can grow in value and generate wealth independent of salary income.

ETF (Exchange-Traded Fund)

A bundle of stocks, bonds, or other assets traded like a single stock. Offers instant diversification and low costs.

Financial Freedom

The stage where your passive income exceeds your expenses, giving you control over your time and choices.

Financial Literacy

The knowledge and skills needed to manage money effectively—budgeting, debt, investing, taxes, and risk management.

Inflation

The gradual rise in prices over time, which reduces the purchasing power of money.

Insurance

A contract that protects you financially from unexpected events (health issues, accidents, property damage).

Liability

Anything that takes money out of your pocket, such as credit card debt, car loans, or a personal residence that generates no income.

Lifestyle Inflation

When income increases and spending rises at the same pace, preventing wealth accumulation.

Net Worth

The total value of your assets minus your liabilities. A key measure of overall financial health.

Passive Income

Money earned with little ongoing effort, such as dividends, royalties, rental income, or online products.

Real Estate Investment Trust (REIT)

A company that owns income-producing properties, allowing investors to buy shares and earn from real estate without direct ownership.

Return on Investment (ROI)

A measure of profitability: how much you gain compared to how much you invested.

Risk Tolerance

Your ability and willingness to handle investment losses without panic.

Scarcity Mindset

The belief that resources and opportunities are limited, often leading to fear-driven financial decisions.

Side Hustle

A secondary source of active income outside your main job, often used to test business ideas or accelerate savings.

Stock

A share of ownership in a company. When the company grows, the stock value and potential dividends grow too.

System

A process or structure (often automated) that manages or generates money without requiring constant human effort.

Taxes

Mandatory payments to the government. Smart planning can minimize taxes legally through deductions, investments, and retirement accounts.

Umbrella Policy

An insurance policy providing extra liability protection beyond standard home or auto coverage.

Wealth

Measured not just in money, but in **time**—how long you can maintain your lifestyle without actively working.

Thank You

Thank you for reading *How Do I Become Rich?*

I wrote this book to simplify the path to wealth, making it clear, practical, and achievable for anyone willing to take action. My hope is that you found ideas here that not only inspire you, but also give you concrete steps to build the life you truly want.

If this book helped you, even in a small way, I would be deeply grateful if you could take just a couple of minutes to leave a review on Amazon. Reviews make a huge difference—they help more readers discover the book, and they let me know what resonated with you most.

Your voice matters. Your feedback shapes future editions, and your story could inspire someone else to take their first step toward financial freedom.

☞ Head to Amazon and share your review — it doesn't need to be long, even a few sentences go a long way.

From the bottom of my heart, thank you for joining me on this journey. Here's to your growth, your freedom, and your version of "rich."

— *Eric LeBouthillier*

www.ingramcontent.com/pod-product-compliance
Lightning Source LLC
Chambersburg PA
CBHW071721210326
41597CB00017B/2554